AF428699

Sweetness Is True Love

Mimoza Hithi

Contents

Rain

Usually rainy days are boring

They are nuisance

That day was unusual

I felt different, full of energy

I was playing with the rain drops

How much they came and become more frequent

I seemed to myself as a dancer among them

Seeking the right partner

I heard the noise of rain

In the empty and damp pavement

It's true the age is just counting

The heart is always new

Incredible this rainy day

It will remain as a black and white image

Of that autumn covered with lace And the aroma that nature releases.

Mimoza Hithi

Always on your shoulders

I wish I was always there

In your arms and hearing

Heartbeat

I felt your breathing

When I'm with you everything

It is beautiful

When I'm with you the world is mine

Everything's else makes sense

I just called you

You are always my inspiration

You are the music of my soul

You're my constant song

Without you life makes no sense

I want to be your part I want every artery to be mine I ask you to stay in your arms.

Always love you

Before you everything

It seems dream

Before you the soul

Feel the unusual tranquility

Your word is worth more

That a treasure

Quietness this night

Creates your image

The words come from the depth

Of the soul and is heard

Fishmonger "will always love"

Nobody forbids

Its flow, no one It does not require explanation It's me and you ....
Maktub.

Mimoza Hithi

Beautiful Gipsy

Beautiful, sleek as always

Stand in front of the mirror

Sitting on your armchair

My Gipsy Every male wants to be close to you maybe even look at the distance My beautiful Gipsy

Who can be that lucky one

Make your dreams cool

To lure you with riots

And endless kisses

My beautiful Gypsy

You keep on staying

Sitting and thinking again

Imagine who can

To be the one who will enter the heart

Tents of my name

Somewhere in the distance a guitar is heard

The rhythm to which you sleep from

And thoughts without hope

It's the heart rate

Your gypsy has put your head under his hat

Drawing sweet sounds

And getting drunk with the melody The sweetness of his guitar
Dance my Gipsy.

Breeze

A soft blush begins to bleed the hair And the heart

felt craving,

A special blow I never felt before.

Looking 'for you, I wanted you long But in vain seduced himself,
From that feeling of death.

I started to search among your dreams,

Between that breeze

That seemed to me as a lightweight hand

And unloved Like that transient feeling, Forgotten feeling.

Last time

I turned my head back

Looking for your image And again I felt craving.

Dancing with clouds

Azure,light, sun glare

The soul begins to wave

At a slow pace

To the endless clouds

Everything looked nice

Something unimaginable

It crosses the boundaries

And I look like a godson

Between their spaces

I feel a void in the spirit

I feel something really

I've been missing for a long time

I want to be part

Of them and be free

I dance with them and fill it My soul is empty

Fantasy

Time over time reflect Timers coming on me

Beautiful moments with dreams

Return with my fantasy

All the best thing about you

I'm keeping the good moments

On every move you're going

Just saw the new person on you

And realising how much I miss you

No cold water will cool me down

No good words can be good

Just let me go inside your heart

End find the right spot

Beautiful moments can make me happy The world inside me is bigger than my heart Let the fantasy be free

Let my mind go away

Time after time will come And take me there.

Forever with you

I find happiness between

The eyes and depths of your soul

As long as you want, to live

Between the blue sea and blue sky

The wind breeze wants to enter

As an invisible line

And to break through the walls

And the veins of my heart

The bounty of your words

It feels easy and thrilled

Everything sensible

Of my being

I want to know, if you're a dream

Or maybe a false blush

Of the whispered words

The wind was spread in small pieces

Those cops really are

They will once join

And they will create the verse

Of an endless poetry

It's that poetry that will come back In a Roman

And as always you are her author

Titled "Forever with you".

I miss it

I feel your breath

Even though you are not with me, I feel your voice, like resounding
Of waves on that clear night.

....

Somewhere a bucket was heard

It was the light breeze of the wind

That resembled your voice

It was your eyesight that made it clearer That night watchman.

....

I asked my heart for explanation

I demanded a retribution soul But they were left with their homes
As a reminder of a diary left in oblivion.

....

Who the dance was the culprit

Nobody knows The fault is always orphan He leaves on a path
without return.

....

The zest for that night

It turns me in time

Then when the dreams were real

When the soul sought light

But everything got fired, went

Leaving behind your memory

And the keyword in my bosom I miss

I'm not perfect

Walking in the morning breeze

And I repeated the word "Anxiety"

Every cell of my body is covered

Anxiety for years

I urge you to jump and walk freely

I demand any feeling to be out of life Blues and the freshness of the sea

I want to be my eternal medicine

Life denies you with its laws

It is unreasonable

And when it checks

You're unknowingly mistaken or you're okay

Judgment on your sins

It never runs its course

Like a malaria that does not exist

Exhausted, like the ghost of a dark one

And "Anxiety" again invades

My soul is dead

Like my own separate life

Between two endless ways

Innocent

I'm looking for a nonsense

Let no one hate me

Let no one judge me

Judgment always requires facts

It requires punishment

Of that act you never did

Innocence,punishment,preaching

Everything that wraps over you

You're the judgment,the justice

I'm sorry that the light of the moon

Requires delete

The condensation of evil

You will always win

The sow of soul,seek

Place to go,and around the veins

Your blood is straight

Oxygen,bad air pulls out

That's right

Where do everyone go?

Which deserves

And you will be innocent As always.

Look through my eyes

Truth is a strange thing

To see you through your eyes

Understanding the silence and trembling

Theirs in certain caste

I'm sorry

With the wave of life,

I'm hearing the sound

My inner voice

And still hesitate

Silence and silence

It turns into persuasion

Where does the body meet and

Freezes every feeling and with

Returns to ice

Everything about me

It is solid, unobtrusive

Looks like an ice, which

It will never break

Someone called my name

But the rigidity of the soul

It's inevitable

She passes her eyes and eats

My body

Search the magic wand

I hit you on my body

And everything comes back

As we do

Live happy ever after.

My city

Somewhere sitting in a cafe

Breathe people's movements

In my city

The truth is beautiful

But lousy

There was rain, a light breeze

It started to float the trees

And with them and

The cadre of the people they held in their hands Fewer under a shelter

A boy's voice was heard

Who sold flowers,

Come on flowers and roses

For lovers

It was February 14, Shen Valentini

Approaching a young boy I got a rose

The ladies of that cute girl

And aesthetic

Another guy was sitting on the sidewalk

And playing in the violin

People crossed for a few moments Listening and giving something in the mark gratitude

Some others talked loudly

While waiting for the next train

A little girl bore her dog

And she asked her mother How long Will the train get back ???

Mom responds a bit

This is a piece of my city Its noise feels strong As a full life artery.

My soul is suffering

Who does not understand the pain

It can not be called alive

Who knows how to relieve it

It is devoted to craving

Someone called my name

And it came to my heart

Like light breeze

Like the dew of the morning

You came suddenly to me

You asked for everything impossible

It was possible

And I believed you got it

The presence of that night itself

Become the witness of our parting

Without my cause and suffering

The times passed and the soul

He needed healing

Someone give me a rose

Then when I needed it

For a word, for a tip

Then when every feeling came to an end

Then when someone left

That rouge will remain the memory

That endless night, like a dream of dreams

Open your heart

Open your heart and let me in

within it

I ask for a place nobody had before

Your veins bleed

On the walls of your heart

Desire and commend

Liberate the heart and seek freedom

That freedom that has been lacking much

Get out of your mind, out of that will

You've been twisted for years

Take away anxiety, horror

That's gonna get you all

Remove the darkness that you are

Involves in its whirlpool

Live that life is expensive

I hope dreams are for you

Destroy that force

To make the soul dark

And she wants to get into the labyrinth

Without end, without leaving, without hope

Where darkness is in place

Open your heart and seek revenge

Let the soul defend itself in the grasslands

Of happiness, in the paradise to which only

You've seen it

It's time to say the suffering stopped

It's time to say to yourself living It's time to feel free It's time to love.

Pain

If you do not crack it out

I know where to find strength to live

Pain has a limit

Even the tears need to drain

I ask for explanation for it

It makes me feel grateful

I want to find the right

Over the dark past

I urge you to break iron wrought iron

I demand payback for the lot

Flush

For the tear that suffering shows

I look for the face of the world

To tear, I'm asking for the silence

It prevails

No one answers you

No one my voice is coming

Lot that flows into the face It is the fact of that pain The soul lives.

Mimoza Hithi

Poor with rich heart

I see suffering, tears, bitterness

Anxiety hungry, in his eyes

And I ask for the world

To tear my thinning

He stays somewhere

In a corner of the groove

And it follows every move

Of people, cars,

Conversations to strangers

Looks like it and it does

Part of this time flux

But in vain, the hunger does not let it go

To get up, the body shakes

He cursed himself

And with his dark fate

The one who is the cause

Of that hunger

Sweetness Is True Love

Someone passes and throws

Some small penny's

raises the head and above the bad luck of that day

Looks at the face of that creature

He was his child

Take his eyes and put his head Still more under his old jacket thank
you for it The tears began to flow over the face and stuffed it in itself
"The Passer" left and he started crying again

Drowned in tears of tears

And he was killed by the humiliation of time.

Mimoza Hithi

Road without return

Sunset had fallen unconscious That day was very busy

Like my own thoughts Evening was coming quiet though some clouds appeared

The sky was clear and blue

Different from me

Immersed in the labyrinth of thoughts

On the no return path I had started

I wanted to shine

I wanted to get rid of myself

Maybe I was wrong

Maybe I didn't had other choice

These were the questions to myself often

I was addressing it but did not find an answer

That's the way I started

It was without return

It was the answer I was asking for

Among my questions

It was the significance of this path without return.

29

Mimoza Hithi

The dream

I travel between dream,

And I'm looking for her

I seek out every detail and fantasy

I look for reality

I seek the end of that tyrant

It always happens to me

Still and taller

Like dreamy ones

Between dream and reality

It's just an internal voice

Which requires the last push

"Launch the road without turning"

Listen to the voice of the soul

And come out in the light

Follow the end of the tyrant

And seek breathing

Who can be a guide?

Who can be triumphant?

No one, but you ..... That light at the end of Tyrant You are expecting you .....

Mimoza Hithi

The feeling of being Mother

I cried when you were born

It was a feeling of joy

It was something I never tried

Before, as a scapegoat that soul

Warm it and give you hope to live

Months, years passed and again

You remain the spy of my soul You remain that unattainable feeling

brilliant

Always the word Mother

In your mouth gives a sense

My life, that life without you

There would be nothing

I love you son

O the most precious

Of my life, a pearl Full of light.

The melody of my life

Somewhere a sound is heard

It is melodies and passerby

It's the silhouette of a kiss

Continuing a dream to leave the whole

You came so suddenly in my life

Together with the aroma of the roses

With the cool breeze of autumn

He just entered

Always on the background

The same sound is heard

Listen to the same musical note

It is the only image that comes to mind

Are you an angel, or devil

That wants to erase Or give a light to my life Tell me !!!!

I hear your voice on the phone

And wonder Who can be

Whoever wants to break my sleep

Again the melody continues

With the same rhythm

With the same note

And again ask for an explanation

But always

It will remain the same

The melody of my destiny The melody of my life.

The Music of the Soul

Somewhere in the background is heard a sound

A note is played

Suddenly I felt craving

I felt the spirit tremble

And the heart beats you

I thought I would never look at you

I thought I would never felt

Your smell

I forgot everything that belonged to you Sometimes that feeling comes and goes away

That feeling which my soul invades

I want to close my eyes and be invisible, fly and just fly

I try to forget all day

Of course this would happen one day

I urge you to get away from my heart

Which still suffers

I set the music of the soul to listen

That melody that is played for me

She knows magic that cleans my soul

It notes has a name

It's the name he wants to give me

Strength to live and heal the open wound with the melody of his word

It's someone who requires that light

Only hope to me

Melody still heard distant

But his word is magical

"Live," Love yourself "

Love ♥

Love is beautiful and free

Like a bird flying in sky

Like a cup of spring water

Like a mountain view

I want to be in your arms

To feel your heart

To look after the beauty

I want everything of you

You're lips are like fresh water

The colour is like red wine

You're spirit is like a treasure

The love for you will last long

Let me go inside you

And get the freshness of the morning

Love comes on strong

To reach the moon and come back.

Elegance

She always wears them

Short dresses

And with her elegance

To leave you speechless

The scent of the body was provocative

The high heels were knocking

We sideways create

The rhythm of a symphony

The rain drops were transformed

In twinkling light

Where did it even get better?

Her image

Everywhere I go through that road

Her shadow appears

I will always remember it Flavour, and elegance.

Prisoner and shadow

Sometimes someone told me

Do not believe in love

Do not let the spirit to the grill

Do not imprison yourself

Her slave,

Let the spirit fly free

And find what you are looking for

Between cage and darkness

I need some light

But in vain, nothing is possible

I wanted to get rid of the slave girl

Much time

I wanted to find that feeling

He was inside me

And it was frozen with time ago

Every moment I looked at a prison

Where did I know that I would not go out with

I decided to close my eyes

Forever and looking

Something I missed for a long time

In the full darkness of that night

I felt only the scent of your perfume

And the constant kiss

I missed a lot ....

You were there !!!!!

The dishonesty!!!!!!

Imagine

There are times when you are dreaming about not being

Sleeping

There are times when imagination goes beyond

Any forecast and return to one

A sting that shakes every artery

To heart, and turn to zombie

I seek explanation, and

I can not

I find the solution of the equilibrium

Which is becoming more and more difficult every day

Equation which started only then

When I started to understand more about life

And for what I feel guilty

Life really is strange,

It is unknown where to start and with whom And when it finishes
and with you ....

Spirit

I would like to get inside of the soul

And a place where nobody sees

Where his quietness gives me

More horizons and warmth

I would love to pass again

Through his labyrinth And never turn back

I often wonder Maybe would have i gone back And cure the soul ?

And the answer is NO ......

The Spirit Is Innocent

And it leaves such

I'm sorry couldn't love you

I'm sorry i couldn't love you

i wish i could loved you

Blame it on me

Forgive me God , you'r servant will be

The soul that sins will die

I wish i have the heart of iron

To break through the strange of my soul

I wish to loved you

I would like of the years I would like all the time

To return back for you

But not in vain, time flows

Together with time memories remain

She is the only witness

We are the gust in this world

Time flows

Mimoza Hithi

Lady

Her look was rude

He wanted to know everything

Her pain was seen in the eyes

As a vision that day

Suffering had become strong

They were visible to us

Wrestling wrinkles

How much they came and increased

The tears you have shed and continue

To flow between you and your eyes

There is another meaning

It's another journal

Everything in this world

It's part of your suffering

Everyone has a fault and must be tried

But more her name "Lady"   45

Mimoza Hithi

Conor's of age

I was actually desperate when I arrived

Fifty, I said everything ended

Hem I was wrong a lot Now life began

She is beautiful, and colour full

Every age has their own distinction

Every facial wrinkle shows

A pain or happiness

Happiness or desperate of Ages

It does not show the smile or the sadness

But the soul itself feels that

Your own flow of life

Every minute or second of this life

Must be tasted just as it comes to you

Just as you feel it

Forgot the age it is just a number.   Mimi

Ocean

I stand before you,and my spirit overwhelms me You are great and powerful The strength and hub of your waves is really scary

The power of the soul triumph over you Ian the one to possess you

As i am God and slave

Of my soul

You screaming with the power of your inanimate soul And i seat in my spirit

To find what i call silence

Everything flows like your waves Everything vanity like a silence of the suffocating ghost

You are powerful

Mimoza Hithi

Blind

Her beauty was unimaginable

Every line of her body

To leave a wish

Anyone who dreams of it

She lived alone, and looked

To give her the spirit of light

That light that she missed

To see the world, everything around it

Spirit requires consolation

And finds it through

Melancholia, notes

Through a musical instrument

Everything seemed dark

There is light within it, there is life

There are no illusions from anyone

Discovered by her

She starts playing the violin

Sweetness Is True Love

Sounds penetrate slowly

It's the inspiration she finds

Between darkness and light

The melody is astonishing

Although the violin does not have the wire

No object to run But it is powerful that it comes out From her blinded spirit.

Mimoza Hithi

Red rose 🌹

I started reading, the word lines They walked some time slowly

End sometimes momentarily

I wanted to know thirsty as it goes on

The book really is the food of knowledge

It is a concern, a suffering

Or a love written in it

It is a part of life that leaves me half

The time I had forgotten

Once in the middle of it I had been introduced

A rose although dry There was the aroma of that day, fresh

How can I forget that rose?

You gave me with love

That rose always

Something reminds me, a feeling

Leave it in the middle ...., ...,

One song left on half

What's left of you is alone

A shadow is a memory, an image

A note thrown into the pentagram

And leave it in oblivion

You were my first love

You were a goblet that he had

Open petals to flower

You were a spring you did not wait

For the summer to come back

Any kiss, any hug

Tells me more than I expected

And I started writing the song

For you, a song like love itself

Life is indecisive

Harsh and full of darkness

Just like that dress I have today

And like the notes in the pentagram A song left in the middle ....

Mimoza Hithi

Sensation

You love touching my body

And feel that breath taking way

My heart stopped beating

It's that moment when electric fire

Run blu and violet

I started moving my body

My mind goes around

You're my inhaler

You're my inspiration

A subtle whisper breath

On my neck

Eyes finding eyes

Heart listen the beatings

The music heat our hearts

She moves against my soul

Always love is our destiny Prophecies melt this moment

On kiss ,one dream

Turn everything to reality

One dance make changes

Beautiful sight resolves around me.

Mimoza Hithi

Autumn

Every season has beauty

And its Colours

But autumn is special

It's playful how can I call it

Autumn just like Spring

It can be called the season of lovers

Somewhere in the street below the umbrella Get the first kiss

Someone offers you to go to the umbrella

And gently as the rain drops themselves To express your first feelings

Furthermore the roads begin to empty

The wind with its slight breeze

It shakes the leaves of the trees

Creating a panorama , a mosaic

Emotions are many

Memories are added

Maybe it's the first year

From a love that was born

Maybe it's the end of a love   55

Failed Melancholy and Happiness Holds the autumn name.

Mimoza Hithi

Just me

Everything is amazing around

The world with good people

I would like to read there mind And be part of them

I would like to see through there eyes

And understand there filling

Would like to have a magic word

And keep them safe

Always I get goosebumps

When I see people falling

In love and be in love

And have a happy ending

Everything is written in my heart

Help them, feel for them

Be who I am

Make them happy, it's me

The sight of my eyes

I went through the dream, in reality

In the darkness, in the light

Your resounding

Give me strength, to fight myself

Maybe I want to live on my dream

And ask for what has been lost for some time I seek the healing of my soul and the beginning of a new stage

I go back to where I left Where did this dream begin?

Where darkness begins to blur

Where tomorrow will be called reality

It is not the darkest who scares you

It's that inner force

To keep gutters tense

And it only creates a vision ....

Mimoza Hithi

My childhood

Everything in the past

Must be left alone

Childhood memories are so much

Even if you're little

My inspiration started

From one my picture

It's that amazing to go

Back in time and waking the memory

Every memory starts with

Remember crying

Fair seed-time had my soul, and I grew up

Like dew of the morning

All the beauty of that

Is someone special

Someone who was part of Someone who will be forever Mommy.

Love is the blood of heart 

Everything will start with

Name of Love

Everything will connect

Between spirits and beauty For the name of Love

We feel like birds

Flying in the morning

In the open sky between

The clouds and endless spaces

I feel the flowing water

Touching my heart

You and me,with a love of God

Singing and watching the stars

Like a bird in the sky

Always dream about having

You in my life, as we laugh together

Like two spirits in one dream

Like one form upon this earth

Mimoza Hithi

I heard a drum in my soul

Coming from the depth of my heart

I listen your voice in my ear

And see your shadow behind the blue veil

No water can Shut the fire of this heart that suffers for you

The stars,like a candles Give me hope and prayers for you Let go
my worries.

The phone call

Hello,Hello......, ...

Good evening , heard a voice

On the other hand the phone

Good evening , it was really a voice

I had forgotten for years

How amazing it is

Go back in time

And remember the past

Which had created a stack of wounds

Your voice is amazing

He said.......

Hem was also a pleasure To hear your voice

I keep talking , with passion

And the past comes in my mind

How long has passed And how many memories, how much nostalgia she was carrying

I was looking forward to seeing you

To meet you, I felt happy when we talked

While now he seemed to me distant

Like a hymn of a wave of pure sky

It's been long time we're not talking

I said ... ,,,,,

Life is full of surprises

He said......,

I did not really think I would hear

Your voice one day

I said .. ,,,

Nothing worse than going to walk

Out along without you

Not knowing where it goes, What did I say to myself when we split?

But the phone of that night It was more than a map

It was a pleasure to talk with you I said ....

Also, he said ..., Good night ... Good night ......

Lust for one night

She was beautiful and sexy

Every man has dreams about her

Always she passed that path

The scent of her perfume was irritating

Her body left to desired

Her look told me something

I never thought she will be mine

Even for one night

I think I was in one of those dreams

It was just me and her

But this time was real

She come on my arms like a butterfly

Come,come whoever you are

Come even you're breaking my heart

Tomorrow will be different day

Different dreams

You're the music of my soul

You're the melody without voice

You're the wind who got my mind

You were the lust of one night

Lonely

At every instant and from every side feeling lonely and without hope

You're beauty doesn't see it

From the other side of you

Anything that comes and goes Rises and sets, is not she like its a fire left behind alone besides the road And her cold soul

Make your self free from the dark side

God has given you the power to win

On every thought and erase them Putting that force on you

Life is not real,she is like

A jar full of wine and blood

Putting you on taste of course

And let you choose

Putting and letting yourself Down it's easy way to do it

Flapping your wings and

You smashed the last of your enemy

Now the world is yours

And the pain they bring is gone

Now you have the power

And fly to him,never be lonely.

Mimoza Hithi

Want to get away

I found the way to go far,far

From reality

I found the wings of flying

And being a singer bird

I smell the odour of garden I fell the cold wind

I went like a arrow to the target

Without knowing we're I'm going The road was dark and cold

My soul has the light of the night

Thinking of pain being part of my life

Talking to my self,lying down and rest

I'm getting tired of being me

The rain began to fall and it seemed as it was pulling the dust away
from my body

That dust was created by years

And look like a callus,who never

Let me to walk, because of pain

Nothing can't stop me to go ahead

Now that I found the way

The light will be my freedom Will Be my happiness.

Believe

Until I get to know my self

Starting believe in miracles

So many years without me

Being abandoned by reality

Praying to see the sky open

Let my heart on everything

Let fire burn inside me

Take away the dark side

Will stand for myself and believe

In love,believe in happiness

Will call in side of me and let

The fresh air gets through my veins

I only ask God if can keep some

Attention on me

Perhaps the time will come

Perhaps he will recognised me

Want to have my life brighter

Like Sun fill our house more than light

Want to fill my soul with desire

Like a garden of roses Want to believe on me.

Never old

Age doesn't mean nothing

There are some wrinkles

Few grey hairs, and more attention

The soul is full of love

Love in this age is deeper

The melody is coming from inside

The secrets is partners with no one The belief is stronger than anything

The sounds of guitar are bigger

They emerge from the depthless of the soul

And create the image of the past

And beginning of the future

He makes music at night

Being troubled by the one

Were mind has tapped the colours of spring

Break the time and your own deep sleep

His soul is younger and more likely

The voice sounds like an angel in the sky

Always love will makes him younger

Never been old enough to get it done

My soul

I'm the one that wants to be there

Whatever the time comes in

I'm the only ones who don't want

To get the past to be close with me

The real life is that one who is unique

Is my begging and my end

The inspiration is to come out

Like a bird who wants freedom

I found my soul in this world

I been awake and watching it

All my good manners has moved Inside my desired spot

Because I cannot sleep at night I write my poetry , the verses come from within the soul and express Who is inside my mind and heart

It's a labyrinth of feeling that not everyone who sees or feels there is morning breeze and evening sunset There is a symphony at a glances magnificent straightforward

There is waking up from another reality

It's like a war colds, between me and

Another world

It's the best way to get your mind to reality

Drink it down

last night you left me alone i started to feel cold and lonely

My body was telling me "You need him"

Love is like running water in the morning

I thought drinking will make my soul full

Closed my eyes and dream, she send me away

To far from my imagination, and close to you

Make as one body,one soul

Some wine drops on my chest my eyes open again in the empty room without you , your presence does everything to move on my cold body

Even you are too far away.i feel you close to me

I feel your breathing goes on my chest

Be my gardner,be my rose nearest to the thorn that i am

Be my garden angel

I continue to drink wine with thirsty ,thinking of you Where will you be and with who?

My imagination goes beyond the time Since the beginning we wore together step by step,side by side

Mimoza Hithi

Be lost in the dream

I want to be lost ,were my dream send me away

I want to be the fairy , were my dream start

Beautiful moments, luxury sides

Bringing forth wings and feathers like angels;

Between dreams i saw me,

I walk into a huge pasture,the melody of the flute is desire

The voice of the soul begins to scream

Requires that much of which is within me

My soul,my body is dead,just my heart still pump

Even everything inside me is gone

Shadow of my body reflect like an angel's arms

Brings the light back to me again

Spirit go far away, love call back again

When my wings i spread,feel the breeze on my chest

It's the power to get up and go back from your life

Hundreds of thousands of years I have been dust

Spreading on flowers to be grow

I want to see through my eyes

I can see the world through my eyes

I will have all the power to call peace

I want to be the one who makes changes

I want to be the one to walk in The Sun

I am part of imagination who looks blind on my eyes

I am nobody and everyone who want to know everything

Keep telling my self be the one to earn the stars

And walk through imaginary line around the galaxy

The world is beautiful full with surprises and memory

Everyone thinks on different way and express the changes

I drop off in the grass, i like the fresh flowers to smell Even when there dry

Felling inside my soul and my body it's strange

Inspiration is from the same time

I made a far journey into a space and being able

To discover quick enough to make the changes

Mimoza Hithi

Seduce by her soul

The beauty of the soul is like e water running in the morning

The freshness and innocence make her more beautiful then ever

The morning sounds, the true love is the treasure

The repentance of her eyes showed sheer quality

She was someone who gave hop to live

She was slave of fragile thoughts

Her passion makes the old vision new

His heart was seduce by her soul

Her body moves make him drunk in the empty glass of wine

Her lips it was like a source to add thirst

His heart was falling for her

Love resembles with fountain where the water flows clean

Love comes on strong on everything

She always risk anything and gat nothing Love gambles away every gift,except her soul.

The voice of the sea

Hearing the inside voice of a Sea

Close my eyes and being suspicion

Resounding of the waves ,requires something to say

Invites me to the depth of the Sea and give inspiration

All the treasure at the bottom of the Sea calls for explanation

Listening the sirens singing with the magic voice

Creating varied and memorable symphony

Creating imagine of glittering pearls

The beauty of the nature,it's valuable treasure

It's open mind between known and unknown

Will free the mind and be part of knowledge

Truly it is the water,who surprise with his voice

Mimoza Hithi

Silence kills

Why the life it's not fear some times ????

Makes you suffer and pain

Filling desperate and without hope

The best way to fight is silence

Praying in front of the God for blessing

Cleaning the soul from sins

Let the the happiness to enter in your spirit

And be part of clean mountain fresh ear

My souls spills into yours and is blended.

My anger makes me strong and alive

In the midst of suffering ,love gives me straightforward

Tears build a stairway to haven

Silence always kills, she is full of surprises

The soul sometimes leave the body

And fly into imagination to find the case

To find the silence , to find hope

Between waves

Life is not always fear and not settle

Liked it would have to be

I hear a drummer in my soul

It's coming from the depth of my heart

My voice sounds like wants to cream of

My body reacts like incredible strange

Being on that position which everyone

Want to be your enemy

I'm scared and resemble like death

I lost in the darkness of the years

I being part of a life without fear

I'm stocked on the past

Sighs heavily from fatigue

Always bring passion and love

When passion is present

Makes the old timers clean and quiet

Fighting for myself is like winning the battle

My soul has been lost many times

Nobody knows the real me

Nobody knows how many times I've crying

Look between the fog

The vision of that night turns me on

And made me feel more curious

For what I called "Enigma"

I wanted to find the light, and tomorrow

The road seemed to be very long

And the fag seemed to me Like my eyes were closed with a thin fabric Where can I just look the light of a lamp

The image of this night Looks like true.

The years , and dark nights

Of my life, with the cries of internal voices

That require salvation

I wanted to follow that light

It was still and more clearly

With the twinkling of the moon

It's a collapse in the small lake

I thought I had walked a lot

And I felt tired, overwhelmed

But my imagination had remained in place along with the fag

And the false twinkle of the moon

Mimoza Hithi

Part of my life

Leaving is always painful

It's like a shadow to follow everywhere

It's like a light that looks at the end of a tyrant

where the closer she gets she goes

It was that time when I had a lot of dreams

And think every dreams come true

It was that time when I got myself to start a new life, new beginning

Going back to my city where I was born

It was something I never thought

My soul started to the emptiness

Yes, somehow comes the emptiness this existence goes through

It was that time when my life turned around

It was that time when all my dreams died

Everything turned into ice and frozen time

Just God allowed some magical reversal to occur

Women's Fragrance

The beauty and happiness of a woman is shown through her eyes

Showing through her soul and heart

Lonely and heartbroken makes her braver

This invisible or secret thing has many exponential

Her spirit is bigger than a mountain

Her love knows no boundaries

Her eyes turn towards the light of God

Inside her exists a force that seeks to destroy any injustice to it

Her fight is going to be silent

Even though her heart was broken so many times

Women, you're the survivor of times

You're the fluid and the melody

You're the mountain of spirits

You're the wind of many words

Mimoza Hithi

Only God knows

Only God knows how much I love you

He is the witness of our soul

We are the note on pentagram

Who makes the perfect song

We are the wind of change

Our love is strong enough

To break the chain of pain

On this path, love is diamond

I can see between your eyes

The mountain of roses

And you called me "The Fountain

Of magic water"

"What is our secret?" "God is witness"

Our soul has desire and faith

And all the beautiful expanses around it

One day we will find the way...

Mimoza Hithi

Be lost in the time

God is the one who created everything

Let the time disappear

Remember that so much you are forgotten

Be lost in the time

Reality shows different ways

Looks like an unlimited time

Sometimes it's about competition

Sometimes stopping in certain ways

The creation of the illusion of unfamiliarity

Creates an explanation

Creates a mirror between the world and the darkness

Has everyone been in front of her

And see the back of the mirror

Going through the darkness

Clean the way and gives an example

Of the future

Mimoza Hithi

Dance with me

Dance with me until the end of my life

Make me feel worm

Take me to your arms and woke me up Give me strength to love

Blood started moving through my veins

My heart pumping through my chest

When you're touching me

My soul feels like I'm flying back to earth

O heart,what a beautiful flower you are

Flapping your wings

You smashed the pointed spears of your soul

And become another human being

Your arms pouring me down like the rain of heaven

I feel upon the rooftop of this world

You're making me happy and braver

Dance with me until the end of my life

God is the one who created everything

Let the time disappear

Remember that so much you are forgotten

Be lost in the time

Mimoza Hithi

The mistress

She always look at the window

And waiting for him

The love she have inside her was real

At every instant resounds the call of love

In her soul somehow comes emptiness

Praise to that happen over and over again

In her eyes occasionally looked sadness

For years she pulled her own existence out of that

Always wanted to find cause for partition

But again she proved her self wrong

The love was more bigger than anything

Words and what she try to think swept

Sometimes your body nurtures the spirit, helps it grow, and gives it wrong advise.

But her heart was giving her strength to fight And love him more than ever

Soul receives that knowledge,between the truth She wanted to make her self free from at one stroke!

Sweetness Is True Love

She want to let her spirit flay over her desire

And never been calling "The mistress"

Mimoza Hithi

Give me light

I'm screaming inside my soul

At every instant and from every side y

I'm looking for something never belonged to my heart

Resounding the call of love

How could this light be the witness

Like a boundary between the darkness Like a bird of the sea and gives me strength to get to the light again

Life gives me many chances to learn

The light is guidelines to choose from

The haven and reality

The vision come back I'm on real life

Still looking for the shadow of light

What is the secret stays on my life

Become a darker side than research

For the enteral light which is "the light of God "

Our bench

We always sit in that bench. How many memories is coming

I am out of words to describe How much this bench, this place mean to me how special you are

Remember that night when I got the first kiss The wind blew lightly over my face and made my breathing more common

Our whole existence is from the bringing into being

Always I go to that place and feelings unfold more than ever

We are the same as before, our love

It's more stronger than ever We are the mountain of course where the water flows clear as the soul itself

Come, come even we're far away

It doesn't matter

We connect with our love , with our soul

It's the bench our witness

Anything that comes and goes

Just the bench will stays there

Mimoza Hithi

Unrestrained

I want to be the one who don't want to control my soul, and let her be free

Like a sword be without trace of iron

Like e wind of wisdom

The body desires in another way

Always want to fallow my soul

And become eventually like a bird

Who always want the freedom and peaceful life

My guardian angel I need a freedom

I want to be rebellion, and fly in the darkness

Like a free spirit and find the light

Now that you've heard me

Be prepared for change and

Let my mind be opened and unrestricted

From all the time I was going through

Don't be afraid to be yourself

Soul receives from soul

Thinking about you ,flying in your dreams

Be part of the time of our love

Always you become a light And never give up on me

Talking is painful and restless

Our soul receives a connection

Our heart is full of love and never go way

It's our memory, it's a sound

Oh music is inspiration of who you love

Music uplift soul and heart

The song of angels

We listen and fed with joy

We are the wind that traverses the mountains

We are the prisoners of time

We are guilty of reality

Our soul has been recantation

Mimoza Hithi

Unrestrained

I want to be the one who don't want to control my soul, and let her be free

Like a sword be without trace of iron

Like e wind of wisdom

The body desires in another way

Always want to fallow my soul

And become eventually like a bird

Who always want the freedom and peaceful life

My guardian angel I need a freedom

I want to be rebellion, and fly in the darkness

Like a free spirit and find the light

Now that you've heard me

Be prepared for change and

Let my mind be opened and unrestricted

From all the time I was going through

Don't be afraid to be yourself

The notion of existence

People, the magical word of being above the natural

The universal meaning

You're hands today are tight and no words You are looking for solutions if you can not

You try to go back in time

Again reacts, scream, youth

But your power is not enough,

You're a physical and mental weakness

They're speak in your name

They're seeking justice under your name

You stay back with your hands and your tongue tied

Though you are a "Hurricane" anyone would be afraid

Those who lead are wolves

They are not saturated by drinking and the last point

Your blood is pure

Get up and fight,get rid of the shackles

Centuries old and make sure God in that beautiful

And prosperous country

It's time to say "Enough"

It's time to tell who you are

It was the time when we were afraid to laugh

It was the time when we could not weep

A song that played the word Love Fight for your existence ...

Mary Christmas Papa

Always I was and will be a "Papas little Girl "

Remember that time when I was waiting

By the window and praying for him to come home

And give me a big hug

The snow continued to fall over and over again

Her whiteness was glittering

And made it even more glittering

More like endless poems

Was Christmas Eve, everything was wonderful

I remember our house had lights on

Not to much fancy decoration but was Really comfortable and nice

At the moment I heard something

It was Papa, his horse makes different

Noises when it's close to home

Like he said "Hey I'm here "

I couldn't wait until he is coming inside

Run out and called him"Papa you're home", he opened his arms

And hugged me with love

He brought me a baby doll, I was flying from happiness

Mary Christmas Papa 😇

Be yourself

I'm trying to be the one

Who's no longer to except anything else

The one who changed the way

And not dependent on none

The real me is that one who is unique

Who is my beginning and my end

I'm trying to see the acting in other people

I'm trying to find the mister, the hypocrisy

Some people are able to do strange things

They want to change the face of the wolf to the lamb and always

Be apparently from other's

I'm myself, the beauty of my soul

Is the lasting beauty

Every drop of blood I spill, means something

Every sound I make, informs the earth

Every prayer is desire, my heart is full of joy. I like to be my self

Mimoza Hithi

Lovers

Every word,every kiss was deeper

Even the rain can't take away the smell

My lipstick still on you

Your heart is full of love

Lovers it is time to set out ,

Of the world of course

The melody is my soul and heart

It's coming from the depth of my life

Our love is breaking the chain

Our hearts stay in one place

You and I with the garden's morning

And the birds flying around

If you're the Angel who protect my spirit

I'm the morning Mermaid who sing for you

We always going to be clean water In the depth of rivers

My angel girl

You're the best thing happened to my life

You're my Angel, you're my dream come true

You're the only flower in my garden

You're the only star on the earth

I'm the happiest Mother on the earth

Because of you

My heart pumping, because of you

My soul is full of joy,because of you My Angel, my Bebe girl

A moment of happiness, You're sitting on my side

Apparently two, but one in soul, you and I

I feel the following way too

When I see you trying to find my self on you We have to much a like to

Between the mirror and you

I see my self,but more beautiful than ever

Because it's you

God bless my soul with you

He gave me reasons to live

Without cause God gave us being

Without cause, God protect you my My Angel, my little girl

Quiet night

Every space in your body has a note

Every note makes a sound

Every sounds creates a melody

The melody creates a song

The song I wrote for you is a inspiration

Has colour of spring flowers

Inspired by the soul inside me

Called by Love, who is being known by

Thousands names

O Love, you who presents every single note,

You're welcome to many souls

You're beautiful words wrap all the body

And if you're naked notes are the transparent veil

My song will became a anthem

Your own deep soul will return to life

This is my oath of love

This is my song for you

Nudity

We come naked to this world

We come from dust and will be dust

The beauty of the body is exceptional

Who being desired from the nature and human being

Females are the chosen ones for beauty Are the most beautiful human God created, the most wanted The clean water in big fountain

I am a sculptor, a painter

In every moment give shapes on

Your beautiful body's way

But then in front of you , I melt

Between the painting and the light You're more radiant than the sun itself your body's skin arouses the feelings Of the beings of the opposite of you

The mirror reflexes

Life is beautiful when you're happy

The beauty whose image fills the mirror

Of the shadow

Let go of your life with worries

Clean the face of a mirror

Always pretend to be who you are

Even the scars are bigger than your body

They represent the truth of the darkness

They are the past

Between the mirror and the soul

Is the difference

The soul is full of love

While the mirror does not reflect

If you want to clean the mirror

Start behold the darkness

And see the truth

Believe your self, clean the soul

Mimoza Hithi

The power of love

Because of you is the reason

I'm alive

Because of you I don't have

Wander why

This is Love flying through the sky

Love comes from one way

Look through the eyes and

Go deep in the heart and place there Build the trust and faith

The beauty of the soul keep love

Strong and safe like a bird in his cage

When the time is right

That bird of the soul my rise in flight

Love have everything to do with care

The moment you think you wan, you lose

Keep that close to you and win the battle

Love want wings to come

The broken heart 💔

Even the weather was crying

My heart was broken on half

My veins are clot from the pain

I lost on time and froze my heart

I always know it you're never going

To feel this love

This Love was beyond the study of storms

Beyond the emptiness

If you want to improve your mind

Than go wayside and pick it up

I've given up my brain,my strength

I'm going to vanish into the darkness

I want to stop the time and come back To another story to my life

Mimoza Hithi

Strange life

I'm trying to find my way to forgive my self

I'm trying to get power on me and fight

I'm trying to please other's to understand

How important is to find love

I'm only the worst enemy of my soul

I'm the water who caused my tears

I have been tricked by this life

To what I thought I would be loved

I'm being forgotten by God and left alone

I'm being nice to others and pay the price

I'm being known for who I am and be a servant

For the sake of love I gave up wealth

It's the time when I telling myself

Vision, see something I don't see

It's the time of testing something

I never tested before

Find your path and change the world

Sweetness Is True Love

There's nothing wrong to walk out alone

Even if I don't know we're I'm going

I'm the road, and the knower of roads

I'm the triumphant return from darkness

Mimoza Hithi

Between the two sides

I called you on my dreams and you come

I was talking with the moon and she listen

I was watching the stars and they light up

My dream was about you and I want to find your test

Even we're part way, we still connect

All my good memories moved thousands miles away

Let me be in your dreams and meet

Let me be your gardener

No distance makes difference

The heart is full of joy and love

Love has anything to do with it

She is like mother's milk,that nourishes the child

You always going to be in my dreams

Until the day comes

The song of the migrating birds will be

Our messenger

And I never going to feel alone

Because you're with me

Connect with animals

Passion makes the old look better

Passion lops was your weakness

How can be the weariness

When passion is going out with you

You're feeling safe and secure around them

Better than you can be with people

You're heart belongs to the world

When it's sorrowing often

That's another way to connect with darkness and light

Yes you're the one side of finding the connection

It's your beginning and your ending There inside voice sounds like a resounding, which warns the start of a storm

Animal soul receives the most important Connect with people who understand them and attracts attention

Make them part of your mind and see

What isn't your affection to connect

Look through them with the inside of spirit And always open your mind

Mimoza Hithi

Curly girl

I would like to touch your hair

I want to kiss your lips

I would like to get through your eyes and find a place to stay

I'm going to be your servant

In every moment I shape an angel

It just you

My soul spilled on you and I was just teasing your fragrance

Your lips drinking my blood and making me thirsty for love

I'm only one who can test your love

I'm the light and you are my road

When you're finding me you'll never expect anything else

The sea becomes full of diamonds

The salt became sweet as honey

Love me,make me happy my curly girl

Let me find a fountain drink in your lips

The garden of roses in your heart

The secret of your soul

I want to kiss you forever

Those who don't feel love

Looking like a bird without arms

Those who don't drink

Are like a cup of spring water

I want to kiss and be kissed

I want to feel the meaning of love

I want to drink and smell the roses

I want to be alive

I lifetime without love is like

Grass in the hot water,is like a dead cell

There's nothing worse then going alone

On the road with darkness, of thinking I'm safe

Open your heart and soul and be loved

Don't forget your human with blood

Let the past to be taken way Live the future and kiss

Mimoza Hithi

Forever

You and me will be forever

Like old times

Loving you is like a getting oxygen

Through my veins

Kissing you is like inhaling my soul

The springtime of roses is coming

The beauty of the nature is like a garden of heaven

That's the time when I meet you

When our bodies become one spirit

You're soul spills love into my heart

And is bleeding

Enter to my life, my love, and let me leave

In every moment I think of your eyes

And fill them with lights

Always will be together and forever

Asked my heart,she answered me

This is Love, to fly toward the future

My spirit says,what a gift it has been

Forever

You and me will be forever

Like old times

Loving you is like a getting oxygen

Through my veins

Kissing you is like inhaling my soul

The springtime of roses is coming

The beauty of the nature is like a garden of heaven

That's the time when I meet you

When our bodies become one spirit

You're soul spills love into my heart

And is bleeding

Enter to my life, my love, and let me leave

In every moment I think of your eyes And fill them with lights

Always will be together and forever

Asked my heart,she answered me

This is Love, to fly toward the future

My spirit says,what a gift it has been

Mimoza Hithi

Quiet night

Every space in your body has a note

Every note makes a sound

Every sounds creates a melody

The melody creates a song

The song I wrote for you is a inspiration

Has colour's of spring flowers

Inspired by the soul inside me

Called by Love, who is being known by

Thousands names

O Love, you who presents every single note,

You're welcome to many souls

You're beautiful words wrap all the body

And if you're naked notes are the transparent veil

My song will became a anthem

Your own deep soul will return to life

This is my oath of love

This is my song for you

I want to be me

Forgive,forget send your imagination way

Give yourself a chance to breathe

Fight inside the darkness and stand up

Call your heart and soul trying again

It's a battle without fighting,a game to win

Let go all your worries and be just You

Let your soul get warm

Breathe in the morning fresh

I'm here drinking alone and thinking

For all my life , with worries and happiness

Thinking about what isn't done right

My heart has fallen to ruined

Giving my self a chance to find a light

Pulling my self out of the river

With abducted waters

And clearing my mind to get the fresh start

Being my self

Mimoza Hithi

Forever

You and me will be forever

Like old times

Loving you is like a getting oxygen

Through my veins

Kissing you is like inhaling my soul

The springtime of roses is coming

The beauty of the nature is like a garden of heaven

That's the time when I meet you

When our bodies become one spirit

You're soul spills love into my heart

And is bleeding

Enter to my life, my love, and let me leave

In every moment I think of your eyes And fill them with lights

Always will be together and forever

Asked my heart,she answered me

This is Love, to fly toward the future

My spirit says,what a gift it has been

I want to kiss you forever

Those who don't feel love

Looking like a bird without arms

Those who don't drink

Are like a cup of spring water

I want to kiss and be kissed

I want to feel the meaning of love

I want to drink and smell the roses

I want to be alive

lifetime without love is like

Grass in the hot water,is like a dead cell

There's nothing worse then going alone

On the road with darkness, of thinking I'm safe

Open your heart and soul and be loved

Don't forget your human with blood

Let the past to be taken way Live the future and kiss

This is Love 💕

This is Love, to find the way through darkness side

To find the existence of light inside the soul

To be inspired by this circle of life and see your self Love is illusion of life , it's the biggest fear

Love comes and goes but the moments stayed

Open your heart and soul and be the first

To tell anyone who is the winner of your heart

I spoke louder your name, and you listen

My soul connect with you in many ways

My heart has fallen into a light

Let me win and be forever yours

Happy Valentines Day

One rose, and the light of the soul

One kiss, and a open heart

Whisper in the wind of joy

The sounds of love

I found you in my dreams

I will never let you go

The power of your soul is full of love

It is the connection of my life

Not many words may describe you

I am a Pictor , a sculptor

In every moment I shape in idol

But in front of you I melt them down

Every breath I release is because of you

Every word I say is your name

My heart has fallen

Happy valentines to my beautiful lady

Mimoza Hithi

Dancing with water 💧

Close your eyes and kiss me

Open your heart and love me

Put your hands around me and hug me

Take my breath away and make me happy

Oh don't sigh heavily from fatigue

The pain of love it's going

The body became the soul

The innocence has been lost

I knew I was in the dream and I would never wake up

Emptiness covering my soul

And feeling more and more

Coldness of water in my imagination

Now is the time of silence

If I dream about him then he was real

Now is the time to swim from the dream

And come back to my real life

Some love we want

There is some love we want with

Our whole life

Open your heart,and the love window

The stars won't use the door, only the light

Will go through the window

Love is the way that free your spirit

From darkness and illusion

Love doesn't know sadness , love is the morning light, love is the

soul's

Through your eyes, I can see your shadow

Your beauty

I can see your lines of your body

There is a candle in your heart and

Want to be lighting ,there is a spark to light the flame

Mimoza Hithi

Melody of the forest

The sounds of the music was incredible

Birdsong was the morning symphony The interplay between music
and melodies of the forest was magnificent

The smell of the forest was so controversial as I was drunk within
The lights that the sparks had given were like lighted candles

The sound of the river make my heart

Full of joy, like a cup of spring water

Like bird of the soul flying in my life

End my body becomes wholly numb

The beauty of the earth is the lasting beauty

I'm servant of the God and drinking from the water of life

My soul smell all the fragrance of forest

Talking with spirits

My soul is innocent and pure

Light and darkness are building up

Thinking of years without hope

Open mind to imagination

I'm close to the decision of hiding it Being bothered by years of terrifying dreams and bad experience

Being part of a misery life, has seen a mirror between this life and the past one

Sometimes it is better to convince yourself

And free my spirit

Because my soul has absorbed all the changes

Every drop of my blood is being poisoned

From the time when my heart has fallen to ruins

Start screaming from the darkness of my other side of me Passion fall to pieces and bring back the weariness

My heart breath heavenly from fatigue But I still alive

Mimoza Hithi

Being alone

Let me go inside you and find your worries

I thought you will be with me

I was wrong, just imagination

I feel your empty side of you

You left me when I need it you

You and I, with the heart of beauty

Like a song that's filled the soul Like a wind who wants you in

The part of my life is vanished

Remember that time when you and I

Being one soul, one body

One form open the earth

When someone asked you

"How is you life journey "

Or mention the gracefulness of love

You claim the mountain and dance

I said I like that, but never thought to be alone

Even a sleepless night

Thoughts keep me away, far away

Imagination crosses its boundaries

And everything turns into reality for some moments

Because I can not sleep

I create, put the verses in the white paper

It's a mechanism within

That helps me in my image

All my thoughts gather in a sleepless night

And they are distributed in a certain direction That we speak with the tongue of the pen

I look at the moon

It looks like it means something How long will I stay excluded without the presence of the sun, she asks

Without the presence of that love within me

Leave the bazaar of my existence to ruin stone after stone

Love you called thousands of names

You're the one to fill a glass of wine

With your body's salt

You are the one who puts my brain and body in eternal sleep at the limits of that night

Some love we want

There is some love we want with

Our whole life

Open your heart,and the love window

The stars won't use the door, only the light

Will go through the window

Love is the way that free your spirit

From darkness and illusion

Love doesn't know sadness , love is the morning light, love is the soul's

Through your eyes, I can see your shadow

Your beauty

I can see your lines of your body

There is a candle in your heart and

Want to be lighting ,there is a spark to light the flame

Mimoza Hithi

Life is really odd

The more you suffers, the more she gives

Make you free from the shackles of one

Over time, make you forget

To forget the scratches of the years

They have remained like "Signs "

And they always show the pain

It is unthinkable to be invisible and dark

Now is the time for the silence

I believe I told you about its essence

I would like to fly from my being

And I would leave forever

I knocked on another door

Someone replied

Who is in the door? I heard a voice

I said, "I am your servant"

He answered "what you wants" I said "the hope of salvation"

How wonderful it is to be

Sweetness Is True Love

For a while with those who are being handed over

And others turn their face to the other direction, while others look at the birds in flight

Life without love, to live it has no value

Love is the water of life, and drink it all

Heart and innocent soul

Mimoza Hithi

Even a sleepless night

Thoughts keep me away, far away

Imagination crosses its boundaries

And everything turns into reality for some moments

Because I can not sleep

I create, put the verses in the white paper

It's a mechanism within

That helps me in my image

All my thoughts gather in a sleepless night

And they are distributed in a certain direction That we speak with
the tongue of the pen

I look at the moon

It looks like it means something How long will I stay excluded
without the presence of the sun, she asks

Without the presence of that love within me

Leave the bazaar of my existence to ruin stone after stone

Love you called thousands of names

You're the one to fill a glass of wine

With your body's salt

You are the one who puts my brain and body in eternal sleep at the
limits of that night

Mimoza Hithi

Some love we want

There is some love we want with

Our whole life

Open your heart,and the love window

The stars won't use the door, only the light

Will go through the window

Love is the way that free your spirit

From darkness and illusion Love doesn't know sadness , love is the morning light, love is the soul's

Through your eyes, I can see your shadow

Your beauty

I can see your lines of your body

There is a candle in your heart and

Want to be lighting ,there is a spark to light the flame

Between the two worlds

Maybe it's dark where you are

Perhaps the sun is different

It's a way between the sound you hear

And your presence

Errors collect the dust and form

Your image

I see only darkness, eyes are closed, blinded by the light of the soul

That leaves you

The connection between two spirits

Although far off

It is the most ubiquitous street where words touch

Warmth of the hand, though icy, speaks

The dawn breeze has secrets, persuading "Do not go back to sleep"

Try to drink all your passion Close your eyes, and try to see With

the other eye ....

Mimoza Hithi

Inside the cave

Life sometimes is not fair

The place you're thinking of

Become a dark side ,the death come around

And I weak up laughing ,at what I thought was grief

It's just imagine how scared I'm from life

It's just a dream which comes and goes

But there's no difference between

The real life and dreams

This cave lifetime done in the illusion

Of the present word

The word of fade away at the death walking

The world is kind of sleepy,only dust

Make different ways of weakening

Stay by my side

I'm not sure if it's a dream or reality

I'm not sure if my hand touched yours

I'm not sure if you're human or angel

I know it's only a dream

But there's a different between being dreaming and staying awake

Everything is illusion of the present world

Small piece staying on the side

Always I want you to be by your side

Want to hear your voice sounds

Want your breath to fly like a wind

Want your soul to stay awake

It's about that time when we are old But the heart is still young, and feel that pressure

there is an inner wakefulness that directs the soul

And that will finally frighten us back To the truth of who we are

Mimoza Hithi

I want to get drunk

Take the slow flow of water

To give the image of a string of words

In the pathway once

When every word comes out of the soul, you feel drunk by their significance

Let me tell you the truth, empty it out

Like bottled alcohol,

You want to go, you want to go out

From my life

Like the freshly-washed breakfast that carries the secret

And she wants you to sleep

When you meet someone you really think you love

Feel and seek its aroma

It's a broken piece, we love

Where are the feelings that you expressed

Why do you think about solid things and no life

Love is an old treasure

The value of which has no reward

That cup will remain full forever, I'm not drunk but you are doing
that to me ......

Mimoza Hithi

Key of the soul

Love is the master of love

Love is inexhaustible source of feeling

Love is the morning fresh

Love is the wind of roses

The beauty of the heart carries the worries and happiness

Heart is full of love and joy

Someone hold the key, open and close in certain time

Until the day you give that key to your loved one

Anything is not in your hands anymore

My heart is awakened like a lamp protected by his soul

I am his slave

I'm trying to run from the wind, when the weather gets worse

Always after the storm will come to a fountain

And finding your soul, who will nourish my heart

Connection

God created existence between us

The pours of soul is incredible to

The bridge connection is called Love

Love is the water of life, it's a light inside of darkness

Happiness comes from passion

Two hearts always finding connection

They need to be able to stable and prepared for the fights

We making love, and the stars watching us

As we laugh together you and I

On earth is one place above, and in another image from timeless land

Heaven is not only place for happiness life should be tasted even here on Earth

The power key is Connection, is the light of the soul

Mimoza Hithi

Blame the soul

How should the soul be shamed

And get wings to flying

When we're here and soul arises

From the ocean so cool Into the sea

Fly, fly o my soul-bird

Travel from the river to the earth And spread your wings around the clean water of happiness

How long I'm going to be blind

And never see the light

How long I'm going to be deaf

And never hear my soul

For how long shall I be in the dust-world

Let's clear my mind, and call out the soul

Follow her rules and make changes

I have the grace of the answer I know the question as well not blame the soul....I'm.

About the Author

Mimoza Hithi was born in Albania, Southeastern Europe. She is a mother of two grown kids. Before she started publishing, she got a graduate degree in the medical assistant program. This is her third book. She spends her free time writing.